ROMANCING GRAVITY

Romancing
GRAVITY
poems

DANIEL ROMO

SILVER BIRCH PRESS
LOS ANGELES, CALIFORNIA

ISBN-13: 978-0615809434

ISBN-10: 061580943X

Published by Silver Birch Press

Web: Silverbirchpress.com

Contact: silverbirchpress@yahoo.com

Cover Photo: DWP, Used by permission

Page 2 Photo: Daniel Romo

Book and Cover Design: Silver Birch Press

Mailing Address:
Silver Birch Press
P.O. Box 29458
Los Angeles, CA 90029

CONTENTS

How did God manage to hide eternity in such obvious places?
DEAN YOUNG

STICKBALL

Summers were a never-ending 7th inning,
and games stretched into the next day
when the sun no longer lit the cul-de-sac.

My brother's knuckleball was an
experiment in flight pattern,
a taunting array of speculation:

> juking and jutting,
> a hovering slow-dance
> > inventing new steps
the batter could never learn.

My fastball was a humming blur of rocket science.

And whoever made contact deserved to
commandeer the moon.

The neighborhood kids were filler.

Portuguese soccer-playing
perpetual strikeout victims
always stuck out in right field,
because they were more skilled with their feet
than with their hands.

Today it's the bottom of the 9th inning.
Two outs.

And we are dreamers posing as fathers
reminding our own children,
"Point your toe to the target.
Keep your elbow up.
And follow through on the pitch."

Today I remember belting an old tennis ball
over the neighbor's roof
into his backyard,
gliding around makeshift bases
with glorious fists raised
as if God was pulling our hands.

LISTEN

For Marty

We called Tommy Manson *T-Man* he was so cool;
it made him sound like a black dude.
Because there was nothing cooler than black dudes in '92,
and Tommy was the frostiest white boy in the school.

On that Saturday night I was feelin' pretty fresh myself,
flossin' in the back seat of Tommy's ride, along with Marty.
Brian, shotgun. Cherry *IROQ* bumpin' through
Buena Park broadcasting to all traffic on Beach Blvd.,

"Beware of Gahr High baseball badasses!"
We took turns freestylin', creating credibility
like we knew what we were doing.

Chillin' after dark
Crusin' Buena Park
Heads bob and sway
Listen to what I say...

Windows down and boom-boom sound,
no one knew I was 98 pounds of awkwardness.
Diffidence.
A pinch-running, sacrifice bunting role player,
and this was the closest to cool and stardom I'd get.

But that didn't matter.
Because it was after midnight,
our hardcore hip-hop mantra leading us into
gangstahood of tomorrow.

Marty warned me, "Don't look back,"
referring to the lowriding, midnight Monte Carlo
behind us, intoxicated, full,
like a six-pack of bald Mexicans.
Marty liked to be in control,
so I often humored him.
And now I see he was talking to himself,
foreshadowing his future failed
marriage.

But I did look back,
because I didn't hear him—eardrums flirting
with bursting, and because I wanted
to always picture the best times of teenhood.

Today, when my wife asks me to
take out the trash or feed the cat,
I pretend I don't hear her the first time.
Maybe I actually don't. But it's worth it.
Eventually replying, "Yes, Dear,"
talking under my breath...

Boom-boom sound
Badass on the town
Buena Park night
Everything, aiight.

AN ACT OF SURRENDER

The bustylicious blonde swimsuit model
who moonlighted as a newscaster
reported it was a carjacking:
a desperate man driving a stolen sedan
leading a fleet of police down the 405,
while the helicopter above
highlighted the high-speed pursuit
as if spotlighting opening night
at the Hollywood Bowl.

The Devil Rays were murdering the Angels
so I switched to the news
hoping to catch tomorrow's forecast.
    That's what it's come to for me,
        deciding on shorts or pants, tank top or polo.

I watched cheering him on,
as he weaved through the glowing lanes
like the sirens were merely shrill reminders
guiding him on the expressway to escape.

We weren't so different:
    him sweating in bucket seats in a car that's not his,
    me slouched into a La-Z-Boy in a life that's not really mine.

Part of me rooted for him to race far away from the chase,
        from the media,
        from this place into a world where the echoes of broken speed limits
    ring like casual conversation.

The other part wanted to see him plow head-on into another car
    jump out the window
        reach for a gun
            engage in a shootout
                with blood and brains and guts
                    spilling all over the freeway
                        so I could be reminded of what it means
to be real.

But I didn't want to be let down yet again,
so I changed the channel back to the ballgame

where men in uniform follow rules enforced
by other men in uniform.
Because it usually ends that way:
the criminal slowly coming to a stop
and getting out,
his conceding hands in the air,
his defeated face
    confiding in the ground.

1.21 JIGOWATTS

Today a sixty-something man zooms past my sedan.
    Last night he came during paid sex
    faster than his Mustang's top speed.
His plugs look believable; they blow like bewildered bumblebees
caught in the fiery hive of the Santa Anas' swarm.
        There is no one in the passenger seat.
                He is smiling as if only he knows why.

Today the U.S. hockey team is down one
in the last seconds of the gold medal game.
      They have pulled their goalie, a frenzied last-ditch effort to tie.
           Prayers become pucks become score.
    Bodies collide into each other as they are reborn,
given new life known as overtime.

        Today a black boy runs after an ice cream truck.
        His rangy inner-city limbs taunt the wind.
        Change rattles in his pocket like
        meager tithes in a collection plate.
        In ten years he will be a millionaire,
        sprinting down European straightaways
        destined to become a track and field god.

Within the past month, there have been major earthquakes
in Japan, Haiti, and Chile. This morning at church my pastor says,
Soon we will all die.

      Today the U.S. lost in overtime,
          settling for a metal shining like a second-class citizen.

Today I am sitting alone on the floor in my living room.
Today I am crying.
    I don't know why.
        I don't even like hockey.

NATIONAL CHAMPIONSHIP

When the star quarterback suffered a separated shoulder in
the first half of the bowl game named after an acidic citrus fruit
and not a fresh, scented flower, he bowed down, planted his hands
on his knees and wilted, realizing his first-team all-everything year
would not have a hero's ending. And when the back-up quarterback
was grabbed by his facemask, pulled into the grizzled face of the
head coach and told, *Just go in and have some fun,* everyone knew
what would happen. How many of us could take the reins, leading
the team to victory at seconds notice? March our team down the field
for the winning score, ignoring the pressure suddenly saddled upon
our shoulder pads. Someday the young back-up blitzed from his
blindside and tackled into the earth's entrails for four uneven quarters
will be a star, parading around the campus, pecs protruding,
conducting post-game interviews thanking his linemen for giving him
such good protection. His mom for driving him to Pop Warner and
sitting in the bleachers all those years. And God for allowing him to
excel at a game he loves. But this was today. And the other team had
bigger, badder linemen. Brutes nasty enough to eat their mothers
whole, spitting out their seeds, ensuring no nice bones from the
family tree would ever grow inside their bodies—probably pretty
goddamn good at it.

CONTAINMENT

She says the sky is on fire. The blue actually cool hue
of the quintessential flame, and clouds: spectators to record
the calamity. There are no such things as planes. They are
products of chemtrails—governmental spaying and neutering.
Airports: kennels/accomplices. She says birds are a dying breed
of matchsticks, striking the fuse with the tips of their beaks.
Runaway balloons are the severed grasping hands of children,
inflated aspirations set ablaze 'round campfire songs gone awry.
Kites, are kites. Mostly pointless. Reigned in when fear outweighs
risk. But fireflies are real: embers of tossed cigarettes thrown over
cold shoulders. She says either way, we'll all burn in hell.

FOLEY

The Black Knight unsheathes his sword before
beheading the fallen hero.
The sound of grating metal is actually a spatula
scraping sidewalk.

The school bully repeatedly punches his victim
in the gut.
The winded "oomph" his body produces
is made by a man behind the scenes striking a stalk of celery
with a large stick.

A machine gun massacres a civilian Afghan town;
the fire is simply a sped-up loop of grapes
pelting a brick wall.

Once a year, fireworks light up dark lives,
then disappear,
fizzle out like wishful thinking.
Boom...Boom...
Boom...
The sound of almost gunpowder.
Of exploding stars.
Of forgotten prayers.

CON ARTIST

In another life he was John Rockefeller, and raided trains with Pancho Villa. You first met him at a *Clue* board game-themed party; he was Professor Plum. That night he told you he graduated Yale at fourteen, and began renegotiating the debt of small European countries later that summer. If it weren't for his claim to be the inspiration for Don Juan, you knew him to be Casanova. But you learned he was a liar, cheat, scoundrel—deftly painting portraits of impossibility, beautiful at what he did.

DOOGIE HOWSER IS GAY

When you came out of the closet
in the wake of your not quite middle-age
newly regained prime-time success,
I finally stopped considering the notion
that teenagers actually could be PhDs.
And though I don't know you personally,
I invested my time in your life.
So I take offense to you keeping your true sexuality
a secret from me all these years.
You could've told me,
or at least your best friend,
Vinnie.

And what about Wanda?
How must she feel knowing
her adolescent onscreen boyfriend
faked kisses that gave credibility
to teenage love?

I believed in you, Doogie.
Every Wednesday night at 8:30,
you gave hope to guys like me,
not the best looking or coolest,
but nice guys who stood for something.
    Now you kneel for something else.

And I question the validity of everything I learned growing up:

        Does distance times rate *actually* equal time?
        Are tomatoes *really* fruits?
        Is the Pythagorean Theorem just a Greek code
        invented to satisfy some fancy pants' fetish with the alphabet
        and redundancy?

You lied, *Boy Genius,*
all the way into 90s sitcom lore and
Emmy award show host today.
Any man-crush I had is destroyed.
Because Doogie Howser is gay.

Revision

      Let's say we're seahorses. Let's say our forgotten birthday candles
have melted into coral. Let's say the coral is forgotten, too.
      Let's say the water is repetition. It is high tide. We have washed ashore.
The children scoop us up with plastic shovels.
                  They drop us into half-filled buckets of sandy water
                      hoping to revive us.
Their mothers convince them to throw us back. Our bodies turn to foam.
                          We are already dead.

Let's say we're notorious bank robbers planning our heist from our hideout.
             Let's say our masks are big yellow happy faces.
             Let's say we are bad men.
             Our mothers have written us letters trying to convince us
                    to turn ourselves in.
We rip them up and smile. We were always disobedient children.
             Let's say we're cops who have been tipped off,
             about to raid the hideout.
             Let's say our guns are loaded, and our laughs are loud.

  Let's say we're liars and none of this happened.
      Let's say we were seahorses.
Let's say our birthdays were never celebrated.
            Let's say we've crossed out those times in our lives.

  Let's say we're convenient rough drafts.

PROPHECY

I tell no one about the flood. Impending waves carrying away lives like torrential
genocide—a suburban sea of humanity. Welcome mats transform to final resting
places. No need to take off shoes in living rooms. There will no longer be dis-
parity in the neighborhood between the least and most manicured front
lawns: all will be a wash. There is no time for warning. Noah was
tipped off and took over a hundred years to build the ark. Babies
will be the first to leave. Current is greater than infant. But
grieving mothers are equal to each other. Storm clouds
will win the race to higher ground. Strands of lighting
splitting sky, a close second. Weathergirls aren't
trained to forecast catastrophe and die like
everyone else. Not even shapely young
hips that emit sunrays can save them.
The Red Cross suggests in such
occurrences, go to the attic or
roof. But who wants a first-
person view of their own
permanent submergence?
This flood is bordering
on biblical. This too
shall pass. I tell no
one how I know
this.

AQUAMARINE

At the bottom of the lake is another lake. And at the bottom of
that lake is an ocean. Distinct water quality separates the bodies.
There are children at the bottom of each lake. Under them are
more children. The children are a passive breed. But they enjoy
playing with rusted lures and remnants of bait. Their lips are
bloodstained and torn; always engaging sharp metal. Their eyes
dilate in a perpetual state of amazement, having never caught
their prey. A constant stream of seaweed and trout travels
between each body of water. They mingle with seahorses that
offer the children rides on their backs. But the children stay put.
They know their place; content to cuddle with starfish. No one
knows about the lakes or ocean. No one knows about the children.
They disappeared long ago. But parents stopped searching.
Chalked up their loss to unknown wonders of the world.
Hands turned into fins, but no one ever taught them how to
use them. Sometimes the children get nostalgic. Long for
man-made memories, the permanence of land. Waving
goodbye is an impossible task.

FELLOW MAN

The weathered cardboard sign was nothing novel.
Nor the location at the Carson exit
off the 605. But his message was.

Help laid-off father.
Fresh, ice cold bottled water.
Only a dollar.

I admired him for the candor of his words.
And for his boldness embedding
assonance in a haiku.

The rain wasn't predicted that Father's Day.

I'm certain the man and his dad
went fishing in the Potomac years ago,
the man a young boy filled with dejection
as the uncooperative worm
(not wanting to die)
squirmed off the hook countless times.

I'm certain his father
gently grasped and lifted his son's head,
looking the boy in his eyes
the color of anticlimactic sunrise
telling him not to give up,
the worm would soon tire
and have no choice but to sacrifice himself
so *his* son wouldn't die
such a slow, writhing death.

Because the man paced the embankment
waving frigid bottles next to
unsympathetic thunderclouds
baiting motorists stopped at the red light,

while drivers nervously fumbled
with their presets,

as if they'd never been thirsty
in all their lives.

TEE BALL

I set the ball the size of a clenched fist
on the tee.
Our front lawn is Fenway Park.
My daughter plays her first game in three weeks:
the beginning of where my junior college dreams
left off.

Keep your eye on the ball.
Hold your hands high.
Swing all the way through the zone.

Her kindergarten teacher says she's the top reader
in the class because she remembers
everything.
Coach said I'd never make it because I lacked
fire.

Her blood is pyre and pine tar.
Her follow-through an eager spark,
a concerted crack condemning my elbow
for not getting out of the way fast enough,
destroying it like remedial sight words
assessed on her first days of school.

Today I'm going to the doctor.
The swelling has not gone down.
But I'm glad she made contact.
Swinging and missing
runs in my family,
even when the ball's set
right on the tee,
like a flaming apple
glowing on the edge
of a teacher's desk.

LITTLE LEAGUE POSITION PRIMER

Pitcher (1)
Often the biggest and most talented. Best arm on the team. A steady
fastball, a heady game. Wise beyond his age. Perennial All-Star.
Nothing to do with the fact that he's almost always the coach's son.
Also one of the strongest hitters and will continue to be so until
college. Plays short when not blowing away tweens in the summer.
Plays quarterback and walks with his pretty girlfriend over vermillion
leaves during the fall.

Catcher (2)
The burliest, sturdiest boy. Squats down for six innings because
twelve-year-old tendons never tire. Checks the hitter's eyes to make
sure he's not stealing signs, and flashes fingers that flicker like
flashlight. One: heater. Two: curve: Three: "The (insert pitcher's first
name) Special."

First Baseman (3)
The biggest boy, but never pitches because his balls skid in the dirt
more than they split the strike zone. Able to stretch and snag throws
over his head with gangly arms that dangle at his side like awkward
apologies. Throws headed towards Toledo. Often the clean-up hitter.
RBI machine who the opposing parents claim, "Has gotta be at least,
fifteen."

Second Baseman (4)
Scrappy kid with a heart bigger than Wrigley Field. Golden glove that
gobbles up grounders. The first one to cry when the team loses. The
last one to change out of his dusty uniform after the game. Stat freak
who could recite the longest hitting streak of every current starter for
every major league team. Wears team cap to school and puts his
favorite ballplayer's baseball card under the bill. A weak hitter,
almost last in the lineup, but a slap-bunt specialist. The smallest body,
but the biggest mouth. Dreams of the Big Leagues harder than anyone
else. Counts box scores instead of sheep. Turns double plays in his
sleep. 4-6-3...4-6-3.

Third Baseman (5)
Strapping youth built for stopping one-hoppers with his chest. Cocky
keeper of the hot corner. Hybrid doubles and home-run hitter.
Potential to play any position. Shotgun arm gunning down runners
before they reach the bag. Most likely to succeed at the next level.

Shortstop (6)
See Pitcher.

Left Field (7)
Not necessarily a spot designated for the clueless kid. Slow runner. Not good with grounders. Often fat. But able to handle a bat. Resident funny guy who drives in his share of laughs and RBI.

Center Field (8)
Ideal leadoff hitter. Often the blackest kids, since they're usually the fastest. Speedy child who swipes bases and never looks back. This will serve him well should he decide to sacrifice baseball for other sports. Sports where his lucrative legs slow down just enough to position him for first-round draft status.

Right Field (9)
It's no coincidence it's designated the last spot in the field; also last in batting. Where the worst ballplayers go to hide, and eventually die. Position designated for the subs who (by rule) must play at least two innings in the field. Sometimes these kids want to sign up. Most often it's their dads who want them to play. A ball hit to them is as least a double. Odds are, equal number of balls will be overran or fumbled. The crowd goes crazy at the routine play. Teammates understand who is out there, and find it futile to complain. Never the coach's son.

SAFE

"I just cost that kid a perfect game."—Jim Joyce
(first base umpire who called the runner safe when he should've
been called out)

The umpire blew the call.
Blew history.
    Watched its curveball breath sail away like an errant throw
    from an off-balanced shortstop in the hole
                        over a first baseman's head.

The young Venezuelan pitcher did not throw a perfect game;
ruled he did not beat the runner to the bag
                      at the bang-bang play at first.

And when the game ended,
his manager stormed out of the dugout,
a thundercloud of profanities hailing a downpour of insults—
    while the umpire stood there knowing he deserved
    every lighting-rod word,

like a weatherman facing the camera
who sometimes doesn't predict the rain.

FRENCH KISS

I stepped outside and crisp air mixed with face like aftershave,
despite the painted bramble of my infant beard. It never rains in
L.A., and the Hispanic weathergirl with a waist like drizzle flowing
into hips like downpour, never mouthed words like: *wet*, *positioning
itself*, *down South*, forecasting that my bike ride to work this morning
would be an adventure. I flung my satchel over my back, rolled up
my pant leg, and pedaled away. Violent wind ruffled my hair berating
me for not wearing a helmet. Roly-poly raindrops bathed my body,
transforming my track jacket and jeans into an Old Navy wetsuit.
My tires struggled to hug the road: more like river of Mother Nature's
bitter spermicide. Better to be a nomad trekking the Sahara searching
for the next oasis, a newlywed barreling down Niagara Falls, or an
eager out of shape tourist trudging up the Eiffel Tower determined
to reach the zenith for a postcard view of the Mediterranean. Summer
couldn't come fast enough I thought, as I slogged down the boulevard.
Season when the busty beauty's forecast correctly calls for *hot nights*,
warm fronts, and *rising mercury*, spicy syllables lingering on the tip
of her Spanish tongue, like French kisses in July.

THE WOMEN WHO CARRY RAIN IN THEIR PURSES

This accessory would seem to contradict the concept of their concealer. Blatant water droplets versus hiding. And, although not a preferred look, it mixes in well with their mascara. A smoky wash dripping down the face. The rain rests in their handbags like a coat of pleasant weather. A calm, collected pool of precipitation. Perhaps it's saved to signify a fresh start. Traces of new beginning following a sudden downpour. It might be a safety net of sorts. Familiar conditions for unfamiliar times. Or maybe they keep it as a reminder of their younger selves. To see how far they've come from the nights and days of brazen young girls who openly tongue-kissed raindrops. Stomped barefoot in puddles. And shunned umbrellas. Walking around town with thunderbolts in their eyes, and storms in their pockets.

THE IMPOTENT SNAKE CHARMER
WHO CAN'T SEDUCE HIS WIFE

She tells her husband, "Snakes, are snakes. Women, are women."
He plays his pungi like a Mumbai magician, hypnotizing his reptilian
partner in their street corner song and dance, far away from the
phosphorescence of Broadway, highlighting the slums of Bombay.
He neglects telling bystanders he's not in danger. That even though
he appears within striking distance of a venomous bite, a snake can
only attack at one third its body length. The snake's mouth is sewn
shut so that only his tongue can escape to taste flesh. The charmer
bites his own tongue; there is no need to reveal this. He knows the
snake is deaf to the music. But the combination of cross-legged
serenading and the allure of coil delivering a mortal wound prove
too profitable to disclose. At the end of the day he places the snake
back in the basket, gathers his money and returns home. A cold
dinner awaits him. Prepared by a sleeping wife's hand that only
heats up when her lonely finger becomes a heated python in search
of its prey.

THE CALVARY

Consists of women scorned—standing up for sisterhood
at the first note of an alerting horn. They swing a mean purse,
fueled by vengeance and justice. Several enlist, but not all are accepted.
Members must be all too familiar with proverbials:
the other woman, rock bottom, giving you the best years of my life.
And if the sound of a battered soul crashing to the floor
like shattered stained glass provides too painful to relive,
she must step aside and give someone else a chance to
ride in from the sunset and save the day.

EXCAVATION THEORY

Tell me about the part when we chalked *X's* on our limbs—
dissected the delicate hinges of our anatomy
in the name of Science.
    My lines were straight,
    unwavering archeological sites
    certain of the reward.
                 Yours fragmented, mostly
     virgin theories
         of expedition afraid to go all the way.
But the blade sliced through your bones
as if rescuing the marrow from the clutches of calcium.
     The nerves proved more difficult.
Their fibers sewn together:
a militia of strong-armed filaments.
     I stopped short of cutting out your heart.
              You called me "chicken"
asking, *Where is the celebrated sonata?*
     The bloody concerto?
             You called me "Balk."
     I didn't correct you.

KISS AND TELL
For El Jefe

Tanya
"I was such an ugly kid—when I played in the sandbox,
the cat kept covering me up."

The first female to hold my hand. Mom only turned around and
yelled, "Run fast kid!" as we crossed busy streets, a Mother/Son
Frogger video game. Though she was good enough to pick me up
when the Camry clipped my leg. And my clubfoot that would make
any 8-iron envious healed rather nicely. But Tanya's hand was more
secure than any joystick I ever grasped. That was the last time I felt in
control: swinging her lovely limb up and down in tune to her
happiness as she sang, "Red Rover Red Rover send Robert right
over!" Robert's beefy body did come right over, breaking our bond,
brandishing me a bloody nose, the loveliness from that five year-old
hand still imprinted in my sweaty, lonely palm.

Melissa
"A girl phoned me the other day and said, 'Come on over. There's no
one home.' I went over. Nobody was home."

A junior high Belinda Carlisle. I was irrelevant, untouched like an
argyle sweater beside a Members Only jacket. We walked to
George's Market after school and sucked on cherry Jolly Ranchers. In
the alley where the frosty Mexican boys chilled on their shiny black
Beach Cruisers, I professed my like. She told me to close my eyes.
Her moist lips christened my blistered mouth, no longer unloved. Her
friends followed us and screamed. Melissa said, "I told you I'd kiss
the dorkiest dude in school, so pay up, bitchezzzzzz..." They handed
her their dollar bills and she hopped onto the handlebars of one of the
Cholos-in-training. She changed her name to *Shy Girl* and they
pedaled away deep into the Rio Grande, her fresh tatted teardrops
tributaries to my teens.

Leslie
"I'm a bad lover. I once caught a peeping tom booing me."

My first. I rubbed the magazine cologne inserts all over my naked
body that resembled a hairy praying mantis, ignoring the painful
paper cuts, before she snuck into the tool shed that was my bedroom.
She told me she had to make sure before we consummated our

relationship. She was a tunnel of dust and steam, and all I could think about was John Henry as I hammered my slight body into her during the most vigorous minute of my life. I lay on the cold cement exhausted, feeling more like power tool than man, until she said, "That was AMAZING! It was like being with a woman. I always thought I was gay. Having sex with the most feminine guy I could find confirms it." She put her clothes on and ran home. I found a flashlight and made shadow puppets, my nude profile sticking its small tongue out at me.

Ex
"During sex, my girlfriend always wants to talk to me. Just the other night she called me from a hotel."

She is a haunting extended metaphor. The kind that never ends. Non-stop negativity. Curt sentence after another. The mother of my misgiving. She couldn't tell me when my birthday was, or our anniversary, my favorite color, movie, cereal, baseball team or anything else that matters. She is the second-hand to my years of rejection, a wagging finger chiding me because she claimed my emotions were tangled in words on a page, my existence stemmed from my fingertips, and I needed to be more observant of beautiful things going on in the world around me. "Why don't you ever write about butterflies, sunsets, or love? It's time to start realizing you're missing out on what's important in life. Damn, Poet. Why don't you ever write about love…?"

*quotes courtesy of Rodney Dangerfield

34

SLICE

I cut myself shaving and I'm ten years old.
Who told my mother bangs were becoming on a boy?
What became of my BMX bike?
Who gave a child a razor?

It's tough to see through the foggy mirror,
a juvenile muddled portrait.

I hum *Hungry like the Wolf*
and trace the initials of my fifth-grade crush,
but I can't remember her name.

I nod my head, assuring myself,
"Words will be vital to the rest of your survival,
like love, gray skies, and shit."

The blood drips down as if apologizing to my face,
knowing there will be many sad days.

I wipe it away, but it's a vengeful fountain.

There is no one there to show me
how to apply pressure
to my wounds.

TAKE-OUT

The teenage cashier at the pizza parlor looks like someone I used to love when I was her age—when on good days my face resembled an order of extra cheese, and on bad days something like double pepperoni. I assume she was a vegan since she never bothered to learn my name.

I gave the familiar face an extra dollar for the ride through *Feel Sorry For Myself Lane* and walked back to my car, holding the box away from my body as if a cardboard delicacy destined for royalty, past the gastric bypass clinic—where the round women stared at me from the other side of the glass with papier-mâché eyes, as if I took their hopes in my fist, and crushed their wallflower spirits at Prom thirty years ago.

ATTENTION

You pulled out an extra hundred-dollar bill from the teller. It's crisp and feels like an expensive suit you'll never wear. Tastes like a rich dessert after you're already full. Smells the way midlife crisis sports car upholstery smells in your dreams (the ones where you're taller and have better posture). The patriotic fibers bleed into your fingertips causing everything you touch to be left with imprints of stars and stripes. The paper towel dispenser in the bathroom at Wal-Mart. The salt and pepper shakers at the Mexican restaurant. Your lover's breasts. You wipe your brow in an act of surrender wondering when this Betsy Ross B.S. will end. A liver-spotted veteran walks by and salutes you.

IN BILLINGS

Said he always thought God would come into his life when he was older—
But you didn't. I don't blame you. Standing with his back against the
kitchen counter, he ate a rare steak holding it in calloused hands like fresh
kill. Licked his fingers and belched when he was finished. That was last
night in Billings. This morning he ate a bowl of cornflakes for breakfast
and laughed while soymilk trickled down, evaporating into his rustic
beard. Even his Labrador he called "Moats-art" got a kick out of it,
howling in tune to the man's own amusement. *How 'bout that boy? Hee,
hee, hee...* And at noon when perfectly parted hair, short-sleeved
Mormons knocked on his front door, he dove to the ground like he did
when he heard Vietcong thunder. That was forty years ago in Hanoi, and
said, *Please, God. Don't let them see me. Hee, hee, hee...*

EN(D)LIST

"My father's in the army. He wants me to join. But I can't work for that corporation." Lloyd Dobler, SAY ANYTHING

Manny's on leave from the Army
Says he's gonna see the world
Germany, France, West Virginia

Says it's easy and makes ya buff

Says he's got Thursdays off
and he's havin' fun

Says he no longer has to worry
about drive-bys in the night
and *eses* on the corner that fight

Says he's done writin' essays in class
worrying about whether or not he'll pass
'cause he's gonna be sergeant first-class

Says he's tired of terrible teachers
who were first class dicks
stupid pricks
couldn't think of anything else to pursue

Says no one can tell him what to do
and, and,
and FUCK uniforms
He looks better in green than his whole platoon

He is free to be
'cause Manny's in the Army now.

CONVERSATION

Hooded underneath a freeway overpass late-night, Arthur brags in
East Los limelight, "I ain't never been to no college, but I got a degree
in graffiti," feverishly shaking the Krylon can relishing the rhythmic

ticking tickling his ear, readying to empty the psychedelic stream of
his 17-year-old psyche onto the parched wall. But if this were a college
course, it would be called something like *Advanced Appreciation*

of Our Song: Words White America Doesn't Want to Hear or Read.
The prerequisite: to hurl oneself into a maelstrom of 80's gangsta'
rap, head bouncing up and down affirming gritty lyrics chronicling

real-life ghetto hardships. Nurse a 40 oz. while viewing a 90's movies
marathon where the signature line of each film is, "Either they don't
know, don't sho', or just don't care about what's goin' on in the hood."

But to Arthur college is as far off as Iceland, or the distance from his
street moniker to Wall Street. A voiceless life of invisibility, just another
lamenting Latino held down by The Man with sunny skin and a fat grin,

destined to a life of leaf-blowing, or laboring in fields adjacent to So Cal
freeways, picking strawberries for upper class's cornucopia. But maybe
the class is basic Philosophy, or Humanities, as Arthur says,

*I think ants are a test from God to see what kind of people we are. Check
it. If we expect them to take from us and smash them assuming they're
gonna steal our comida, we're going to Hell. But if we accept them*

*believing they have as much right to the table as we do, especially por
que they clean up the mess people leave, Heaven. Except for red ants.
Them motherfuckers are Satan's teeth,*

before spraying an American flag on the wall, a white stick man in the
middle, eyes closed like death, palms compressing ears sealing in status
quo, ensuring no bug will ever crawl in.

BLOOD BROTHERS

When we were ten
we pricked our index fingers,
strangled them, breathless,
until they became a bloody
Cyclops,
and sloppily bonded them together.

He moved four years later,
and I never saw him
until the other day,
bored at work
succumbing to
Facebook again.

His shaved head
mosaic skull tattoos
and double birds
made it difficult to
recognize my friend.

I recalled that day
in Ms. Barrett's class
when we straightened
and sharpened staples
becoming family:

—The two-story, built-in pool, white boy
—The two-bedroom, blow-up pool, Latino
"Brothers Forever…"

However
the emblazoned swastika
branded
on Kevin's left wrist,
broadcast
we lost touch
long ago.

How to Do Your Makeup Like a Chola

I.
Start with the foundation. Because a steady one has never existed in her life, this part is easy. Apply a base ready to handle any bumps in the road, such as: welts from slaps in the face in the form of stereo-typing before she even has a chance to grow up. A good foundation can conceal any hardships you're bound to endure in the future.

II.
Apply the blush. Brush it on in a manner maximizing the sharpness of the cheekbones highlighting the refinement of the face: exotic, brilliant, like ancestral Mayan carvings. Avoid using too much, as this will give people the wrong impression: clown, slut.

III.
Use the pencil to shape your eyebrows, thin and arched. This will create an exaggerated look of bewilderment which may come in handy should you ever decide to visit the most upscale department store in the mall. You can actually look the part rather than just play dumb, when the saleswomen follow you around as if you stole some sparkly earrings say, and shoved them into your purse (also presumed stolen). The scarce hairs (mostly drawn on) will also serve as a barrier to people looking you in the eyes, easing any guilt you may have for sins committed that could cause your mother eternal grief.

IV.
Put on the eyeshadow base before the eyeshadow so the shadow will set better. Use a shimmery silver to complement the golden crucifix hiding deep in the cleavage peering out from the snug wifebeater. Then blend in the eyeshadow on your crease to create depth. Otherwise you'll be seen as shallow, incapable of accomplishing anything meaningful in life (Having children while being a teenager doesn't count as an accomplishment.).

V.
Guide the eyeliner across the fringes of the upper lid, slowly advancing all the way around the eye. Repeat the process. The thicker the better. Don't neglect the corners—where the liner should harshly extend pointing away from the pupils as if accusing the ears of betraying the rest of the face.

VI.
Curl the lashes. Perfecting the art of eye-batting is vital. You'll need to use your sexuality like a lasso, roping potential suitors (most likely Cholos) who will show everyone how much they care by giving you an assortment of hickies on your neck like a raunchy connect the dots. And in turn get your name tatted in cursive on his neck, forever displaying the bond you share. Because why waste money on a ring of any sort when nothing says *I love you, heina* more than a neck tattoo.

VII.
The mascara should coat the lashes like an oversized Pendleton. Drape it on as if protecting the eyes from any sort of illumination that forces the Chola to examine her current lifestyle. She doesn't need to be reminded that being a mother is more than making sure *Jr.* has the freshest baby shoes. That dropping out of high school maybe wasn't the best move. Or that picking and choosing your battles will give you and your loved ones a longer life span. Because in this *mi vida loca* world of *barrios* and bandanas, it's all about respect, and every day is a battle.

VIII.
Finally, trace the lips with lip liner. Lipstick isn't needed. It would only rub off from your kiss my ass *FTW* attitude. But the liner will still be there. The last trace of any hope you'll have at making something out of yourself.

WHEN IN LONG BEACH

Kiss homeless on foreheads while they sleep on the knoll
in front of the library at City Hall; drink their dreams dry

and spit out seeds from their nightmares. Wipe the soil from their
brows; grind it into skin: tatted euphemisms yet to come.

Tiptoe, naked through the ghetto; genitalia is universal, neutral,
and you're less likely to be mistaken for having gang ties.

Ignore single mothers' cries, curbside memorials,
and barricaded cul-de-sacs. They occur too frequently.

Sift sand on the shore smirking at the sea, once cerulean currents
of nonconformity now jaded, gagged, bound by breakwater.

Sit Indian-style in garages, sifting through "medicinal" haze
lifting to the rafters. And chew on songs birthed from wombs

of empty Corona bottles pardoning indie bands swum mainstream.
Follow the gulls.

They know where the best places in town are
to eat.

PUSHED

He shot up from his desk and yelled,
    "Nasty-ass bitch motherfucker!"
when I told him to leave,
perhaps mistaking my
nervous, shocked smile
for mocking
when he thrusted his hands into my chest
on his way out the door,
as if my classroom were the courts,
and we had just finished fighting
over a loose ball.

It must've been instinctive for me
to wrap my arms around him,
and squeeze just enough
so he didn't hurt himself,
or me,
because I knew no one at home
ever did.

        Even though for a moment,
        I wanted to break his ribs!
        Snap them in half
        because his ghetto-born-and-bred guts
        were too big
        for his 14-year-old body.

And when I asked him,
"If I let you go,
are you going to hit me?"
and he replied,
"I just want you to let me go,"
I let him go…

The staff assistant called out
some of my students to write down statements.
On their way out they said,
"Don't worry.
We got your back."

I wrote down my statement, which wasn't
a poem,
but surreal nonfiction.

And I felt kind of guilty after security found him
hiding in the bathroom.
Maybe I could've ignored his apathy,
let his attitude slide.

Because kids like that
are too easy to find.
      They always motherfuckin' are.

ROOTS

What is the difference between tangled and nappy?
Heads of hair growing on other sides of tracks—
interlocking of identity. Some kids sit on mother's lap:
a post-bath ritual. Others fashion a do-it-yourself do
in the mirror: a daily lesson in upkeep/upbringing.
Some strands become unruly. Flaxen tendrils with
a tendency to stray. Other wisps rebel. Stand out like
stubborn schoolchildren, a label they wear themselves.
Frilly ribbons frame surays, suburban sky the face of
ruptured stars. Elsewhere, rhythmic beads clap together
during double-dutch upon urban concrete that has
witnessed too much. Brushing locks—routine,
day after day, a maintained shimmery cascade.
Healthier than straightening with a hot comb,
chemicals condemning scalp on special occasions:
family reunions, funerals, weddings. Feisty threads,
interlaced. Kinky curls; in your face. A condition.
A lifestyle. Weaving in Sunday Best with what's left
of the self.

CIVITAS

Suburbian

You've caught that simple lull. A halfhearted bated breath. A stale puddle of apologies. It was the season of apathetic reasoning. Wind lightly moved, more than blew. Leaves were uncertain of their status; the rake's teeth were clean. The busty weathergirl's forecast called for warnings, yet she neglected to say what kind. Children did handstands, but didn't smile. Or were they holding up the earth? Windowsills grew dusty and became infested with termites. Even the most All-American apple pies couldn't revive them. Stray dogs roamed neighborhoods in the name of hunger and "up to no good." How were they to know the difference? You sat on a splintered rocking chair, feet planted in the porch. Your eyes—splintered orbs— offered a panoramic view of the city. Somewhere there is a street that deserves to be called *Main*. This is not it. Your cheeks were flush with famine, holding out for hope, waiting to exhale.

Rus Ruris

Cornfields are organic tract housing. Acres of obedient flock grasping towards God. More than just hoping for a bountiful harvest. Hoping is inconsistent with faith. Folks 'round these parts stand steadfast, believing there will be no drought. They wear values on rolled-up sleeves. Keep their hands clean by keeping them dirty. Their words are seedlings nestled in soil. Their actions serve as water. To live off the land is an extended metaphor. To survey the land is to survey the self. Residents pause to reflect on approaching tornadoes, even if when weathervanes are at their calmest. There's safety in wonderment. Possible versus probable chain of events. Silos store best when their bellies are full. Busy slaughterhouses denote sore wrists and bloody fists. When grazing is good, so is the cut of the cattle. Success is measured in increments of excess and tenderness.

Urbis

He asks, "Can I wash your windows?" I tell him, "I ride a bike; it doesn't have windows." I give him a buck, anyway. I know how he'll probably spend it. I also know men thirst in different ways. Liquor stores here are bigger than libraries, and outnumber them eight to one. Librarians do their best to recruit a new breed of readers. But the allure of the same old 40 oz. is oh so strong. Here, front porches are stoops. Stoop is often equated with the idiom, "to new lows;" here, that's an oxymoron. Sons repeat their fathers' mistakes—juniors themselves. Daughters become like their unwed mothers. The traditional family unit is held together by subsidized rent and inconsistent child support checks. Even the sky is looking for a stable home. Over there (which is an extension of over here), brown is the new black is the new brown. Day laborers corral themselves in home improvement parking lots hoping to enhance their lives by rebuilding the lives of others. The lives of others is mostly used in the literal sense. Here lie too many buried similes; e.g., *Catering trucks gleam like leftovers of the American Dream.* Here is where boulevards named after civil rights leaders are regarded as the most dangerous streets in the city. Here is the place where nighttime comes to die until morning. I tell no one, I was born here.

THE OTHER SIDE OF TOWN

It's 1 a.m. in September.
Three witches walk towards me
down Artesia Boulevard
armed with eyebrows like
my father's temper.

I fear witches more than heights,
clowns, and spiteful waiters.

And they're a month early.

I'll tell them it was an accident;
I simply forgot to wash the dishes.
And I pulled out all the whiskers of
the black cat in the alley
because he bragged of his many lives.

My father had one.

Death and poetry
are related in life:
bloodlines of realism so exaggerated,
they makes sense.

I decide to cut across the street,

pushing too real reveries
to the side,
            like horrid vegetables.

SESTINA FOR "THE 909"

In the lovely city of Rancho Cucamonga
where the heat cooks even the coolest dudes' cajones,
lives the mysterious, elusive bugaboo.
Nestled in the San Gabriels, octogenarian
legend has it he wails at night, uvula
rung by a covert Quasimodo under midnight's murky sheet.

My grandmother doesn't believe. "Sheet,
este pinche noise is just Rancho Cucamonga
wind, gurgling like chorizo stuck on the uvula.
Sabes when the scrambled cajones
go down the wrong pipe and you choke like octogenarian
putas giving tonguekisses to nasty bugaboos.

But the residents say, *Beware of the bugaboo.*
At night he sleeps underneath blankets and dirty sheets
of unsuspecting homeless teens and octogenarians,
and blends in during the day with Rancho Cucamonga
sun, glistening rays: his dangling cajones
taunting our dry mouths like a juicy uvula.

The children's teachers assign vocab words like *uvula*
when they should assign terms like *bugaboo.*
But the residents simply lack the cajones
to seek out the menace, sign an official sheet
of paper petitioning the state to declare Rancho Cucamonga
in need of help like "I'vefallenandIcan'tgetup" octogenarians.

It's an unspoken scene, grizzly like octogenarian
foreplay, an elderly tongue tantalizing uvula.
Who can help the residents of Rancho Cucamonga
capture the beastie known only as bugaboo,
this invisible criminal with a growing rap sheet
deeper than the canyons of El Cajon.

Cajonas y cajones,
I implore you to help weed out this octogenarian
myth. There is no hard data or spread sheets
providing statistics for this entity's existence, the uvula
that hangs in the mouth of the 909, bugabooing
the San Bernardino metropolis known as Rancho Cucamonga.

"Let's snuff it out; stuff its cajones down its uvula,"
says my octogenarian grandmother about the bugaboo.
"Sheet. No damn ghost is gonna fuck with Rancho Cucamonga."

SMOKE AND MIRRORS

"*Chisme* is the devil's tongue," Aunt Lucy told me and my cousins
every time she caught us congregated in her garage gossiping about
our 6th grade classmates.

Aunt Lucy, who formerly worked in Vegas as a "lovely assistant"
to David Copperfield (getting sawed in half at the head and hips,
disappearing from black boxes with tight lips), once cracked a raw
egg on my head when I was nine suffering from a 103 degree fever,
mashing it into my scalp with her fists claiming, "The energy from
the chicken's *kulo* will calm the savory spirits simmering in his soul.
"Dientes del Diablo, Mijo."

Who once lifted her third husband by the greasy v-neck of his
chorizo-stained undershirt (the man we weren't allowed to talk about)
hurling him down a flight of stairs, then soared from the banister,
bionic elbow leading the way like a luchadore unmasked by the foe
sprawled semi-conscious, two cracked ribs, and one story below.

Who spent Saturday nights guzzling *Tecates* cursing the TV during
heavyweight fights, and Sunday mornings lamenting the loss of her
only lover we ever referred to as our uncle, rocking back and forth
in the chair he built for her and my cousin who died before we
ever met.

Who kissed my forehead from her deathbed and said,
"Don't believe everything you hear."

Someday during someone's birthday party, or wedding reception,
or funeral, I'll catch my nieces and nephews huddled together talking
about something I got reprimanded for talking about when I was
their age. I'll be the pious Uncle of Profundity voicing sage sentiments.
"*Hijos*. Breadcrumbs are the Lord's dandruff." They'll look at me
bewildered—arched brows bridges to Aunt Lucy's being.

DRIVE-IN

My parents told me I was conceived there during
opening night of *American Graffiti,*
perhaps explaining why I always found Richie Cunningham
cooler than The Fonz,
and greasy spoons preferential to French bistros.

On lucky Saturday nights the Volvo was our four-star restaurant,
the only time we had a family dinner:
foil-wrapped beaming Mexican mummies unwound
becoming bean burrito delicacies during dusk.

Dad stared through the grainy images on the screen
mumbling, *Ain't this the life,*
right about the time I learned what a rhetorical question was,
unsure if he was asking us or trying to convince himself.

Mom commented how the elevated front of each car
reminded her of caring for newly sprained ankles.

My only concern, whether or not we got to stay for
the second feature.

Serrated elbows flew like a maiming game of tag,
my brother and I positioning for the best view in the
back seat of the sedan, as if that's not an oxymoron.
     (Some of the bruises still have not gone away.)

The speaker hooked on the driver's side window
reminded us how poor we were,
as if only one ear worthy of sound.

Yesterday at the mega-gamma-super-colossal-plex
where 3D images leap from the screen
as if experiencing the buoyancy of reality for the first time,
my six year-old daughter asked, "What's a drive-in?"

Should I have told her it's where families went
to get away from themselves?
Or it's the poorman's cinema,
where if you listen hard enough,
you can hear the clanking
     of fallen silverware.

TRANSCENDENTAL HUMMING

To live inside the lava lamp I bought last Sunday morning at the
yard sale from the dead neighbor's stepson whose tulip garden
we trampled retrieving our baseballs every summer twilight
before she'd yell at us from her kitchen window—Little Demons!

To have the Jordan rookie cards stuck in between our spokes
making our *Toys 'R' Us* BMXs zoom faster than the General Lee
and K.I.T.T. combined; even Hasselhoff and *Them Dukes, Them
Crazy Dukes* would envy us—flying faster than Armageddon's
heartbeat down Ibex Avenue dodging soccer moms while the
dragonflies rooted us on.

To be a fiery droplet tickling gravity: aloof compound more com-
fortable in dorm rooms than board rooms, brilliant 5 o'clock shadow
starlets, searing globular metaphorical sinners, Warhol-following
peyote-infused twice-removed long lost cousins of jellyfish swimming
upstream, downstream, mainstream magma mainstays illuminating
the way into pop culture ubiquity.

I was never allowed to own a lava lamp as a kid, because mom said
they were tacky and didn't match the décor. And because she said they
reminded her of the devil.

THE PROBLEM WITH FATE

I.

The problem with fate is that it lacks closure:
the cyclical embrace of karma and kismet
clasped like buttons on small children's
peacoats from the 40's.
The quality of life has deteriorated today.

II.

"Everything is little, kid.
Dreams used to be big.
And the sky was full of 'em."

III.

A young boy (not me) used to
shoot small birds out of the horizon
with a BB gun,
intoxicated with the scent
of coercion and conquest;
watch them stagger, dazed,
ricocheting between the clouds.
"It's just a bird, Mom."
Little men. Hunters.
Gatherers are gone.

IV.

We are left holding the bag.
Its contents are stale.
Perhaps expired cold-cuts
purchased from a delicatessen
in a neighborhood known as Little Italy.
Maybe a greasy taco
bought from a silver pushcart
at a busy intersection in Santa Ana. *"Gracias."*
Most likely it's the crumbs of a glowing dream,
gone the way of Roman numerals.
Sun chips for the soul.

V.

The problem with fate is that it lacks closure
The problem with fate is that it lacks closure
The problem with fate is that it lacks closure

"Dreams used to be big,"
"It's just a bird, Mom,"
"Gracias,"
they murmur,
always having more to mouth.

SWINGS

In third grade I threw Theo Dean off his swing. He soared,
beautiful, more bird than boy. Flailing limbs romancing gravity—
more acquainted with the clouds than any other kid at Kennedy
Elementary. His dad was a paraplegic from a stock-car-racing
accident many years ago, so I hoped Theo would be okay. He was
really good at ding-dong-ditch, and ringing doorbells rolling away
wildly in a wheelchair didn't sound as fun. The ground jealous;
broken arm when he landed. Theo lost the desire to go on the
swings after that, preferring dodge ball instead. I think he races
boats these days. I lost recess for a week, and teach creative
writing now: more cloud than man.

RIDING MY SCHWINN TO WIENERSCHNITZEL DURING MY CONFERENCE PERIOD

I should be grading papers right now,
even though I already know the outcome:
a steady stream of scarlet scores, fragile,
low, like the concern from those
whose apathetic hands birthed them.

I was craving chili-cheese fries,
a manufactured mountain of grease, gluttony, escape.

Ask any poet their definition of escape:

> *stepping outside oneself, AWOL,*
> *always coming back to the source*
> *of inspiration.*

Ask any teacher their definition:

> *running outside the campus,*
> *away from PTA, SATs, ADHD,*
> *never second-guessing or looking back.*

Part of me wants to sit in the
cracked leather chair
the budget-cutting district has furnished me.
Scribble obscenities in the form of
letter grades: an assembly line of procrastination
and consternation.

The other part wants to
sip soda on the fast food bench,
chili-fried legs dangling from my lips
like processed past participles,
contemplating the consequences
if my principals ever see this
in print.

FREQUENT FLYER

They stick bite-size chocolates on the tables
to appease us at our monthly staff meetings.
They show us graphs on degrees of retention.

> *We are losing our children.*
> *We need to plan lessons with more rigor and relevance.*
> *Our students are playing catch-up to India.*

The day before in my creative writing class,
Kenneth Platt asked anyone who'd listen,
"Did you know that we lose 40 to 100 strands of hair a day?
The Neanderthal's brain was bigger than ours?
That India has more sex than any country in the world?"

To which Mitch replied, "Book me a flight to Bollywood, baby."

> *We need to use our instruction minutes wisely.*
> *Students can't learn if they're not actively engaged.*
> *They'll never fulfill our expectations if we can't*
> *stimulate them enough to pay attention.*
> *As educators, it's our job to…*

I stare at the spinning ceiling fans
imagining I'm in Calcutta—
a transcendental passenger reflecting in a rickshaw
letting someone else earning meager pay lead *me* around,
so I can raise my hand and ask,

"Um…What are we supposed to do again?"

BIOLOGY

Because when Charlie Brown's teacher yelps,
Wah-wah-wah wah wah-wah-wah,
she points at the desk telling him to get his rocks off;
females won't fancy such a soiled collection of contaminants.

Because when she proclaims, *Wah wah-wah-wah-wah wah wah,*
she explains to Lucy the importance of acting like a young lady,
and to stop playing outside with an assortment of balls;
boys don't like girls with dirty knees.

Because when she bellows, *Wah-wah-wah-wah wah wah,*
she instructs Linus to stop yapping about fictitious holiday icons
and finish reading the reality in his Science book,
pages pertaining to petrified wood and other hard objects.

Imagine that—rusty dusty trombone voice woman
making such demands of her students.
But sometimes she says things just as shocking:

Wah-wah-wah wah-wah-wah wah-wah states,
Billy goats urinate on their own heads
to smell more attractive to females.

Wah wah wah wah wah wah means, to avoid predators,
a mother Slow Loris licks her offspring with poison
before sending them off to search for food.

And the day she could take no more, when the kids
simultaneously acted out their best exploding mitochondria impressions
she snapped, *WAH! WAH! WAH! WAH!*
The exorbitant number of students failing in school
is directly attributed to the deterioration of the family unit!!!

Charlie Brown got rocks in his bag for Halloween,
because someone has to be Charlie Brown.

Lucy started pulling the football away
(after she overheard her mom talking on the phone),
because her dad "pulled the rug out" from them when he left.

And Linus lies down all night in a field of wishful thinking:
fetal position, thumb in mouth, blanket covering his cold body,
because he's waiting for a *Great Pumpkin*
that never shows up.

LAST SUMMER

We ran Ibex Avenue—
courting the dusk and counting crickets,
before our mothers called us inside
in three different languages for a late dinner.

Paul called everyone *dickhead* that year.
And Tony kissed all three of the Hernandez girls,
even Eva with the mole on her neck
shaped like a churro.

On Saturdays we bounced
a lopsided rubber basketball
in my fissured driveway,
trampling my senile neighbor's begonias,
then drank from her tired hose
letting the water dribble down our scrawny chests
before tossing it aside,
proudly looking up to the neon August sky
palms outstretched as if
we were gods.

When seduced by the incantations
of the Indian ice cream man,
we ran inside our homes, gathering change
to buy Mexican candies
made with trace amounts of lead,
and sweet cigarettes with powdered sugar tips.

We didn't call each other *fags*
for enticing the ladybugs to crawl up our fingertips.
We saved bravado for our dads,
who cursed the TV when the Dodgers lost.
We even cried when I moved away.

I hear Paul has testicular cancer now.
Tony is paying alimony to four exes.
But we were bad-asses then—
lying on rooftops,
humming the song of the ice cream man,
puffing away
on candy cigs.

ORBITING
For Albert

We sat on the curb and bribed grownups for beer.
Baby-faced seniors on a Saturday night.

Adults denied us as if they were the hottest girls in school
and we were who we were.

But we courted rejection and carried no shame.
Our perseverance and pooled funds bought a sympathetic good man.

Good Samaritan who broke laws for the wellbeing of others.
We were well at being young and drunk.

"Thanks. You can keep the change." He came out with a case of
Coronas and a pack of Pampers, delivered our beer, and disappeared.

He, no doubt, a former neglected prom date.
Today the man's baby is almost grown and sits outside a liquor store.

I want to buy beer for the underage boy and his thirsty friends.
To watch them tilt their heads back,

bring the bottles to their mouths, as they look up at worlds
they're now man enough to explore.

ACKNOWLEDGEMENTS

These works or earlier versions first appeared in the following:
STICKBALL: *decomP*
LISTEN, TRANSCENDENTAL HUMMING: *Praxilla*
AN ACT OF SURRENDER: *MiPOesias*
1.21 JIGOWATTS: *Fogged Clarity*
NATIONAL CHAMPIONSHIP: *Deuce Coupe*
CONTAINMENT, WHEN IN LONG BEACH, THE PROBLEM WITH FATE: *Ditch*
FOLEY: *Sundog Lit*
CON ARTIST, ATTENTION: *Poetry Superhighway*
DOOGIE HOWSER IS GAY: *Zygote in my Coffee*
REVISION: *> Kill Author*
PROPHECY: *Heavy Feather Review*
AQUAMARINE: *Penduline Press*
FELLOW MAN, EN(D)LIST, BLOOD BROTHERS: *Verdad*
TEE BALL: *Litterbox Magazine*
LITTLE LEAGUE POSITION PRIMER: *Hobart*
SAFE: *Deuce Coupe*
FRENCH KISS, BIOLOGY: *Pear Noir*
THE WOMEN WHO CARRY RAIN IN THEIR PURSES: *Stone Highway Review*
THE IMPOTENT SNAKE CHARMER WHO CAN'T SEDUCE HIS WIFE: *Word Riot*
THE CALVARY: *Dinosaur Bees*
EXCAVATION THEORY: *Commonline*
KISS AND TELL: *Bananafish*
TAKE-OUT: *New Wave Vomit*
IN BILLINGS: *Weirdyear*
CONVERSATION, SMOKE AND MIRRORS: *Whisper and Scream Magazine*
HOW TO DO YOUR MAKEUP LIKE A CHOLA: *The Acentos Review*
PUSHED: *Martian Lit*
ROOTS: *Blue Fifth Review*
CIVITAS: *Journal of Compressed Creative Arts*
THE OTHER SIDE OF TOWN: *Gloom Cupboard*
SESTINA FOR "THE 909": *Asphodel Madness*
DRIVE-IN: *Deuce Coupe*
SWINGS: *Dogzplot*
RIDING MY SCHWINN TO WIENERSCHNITZEL, FREQUENT FLYER: *Underground Voices Magazine*
LAST SUMMER: *Camroc Press Review*
ORBITING: *Banango Street*

About the Author

 Daniel Romo is the author of *When Kerosene's Involved* (Black Coffee Press, 2013). His poetry and photography can be found in the *Los Angeles Review, Gargoyle, MiPOesias, Yemassee, Hobart*, and elsewhere. He holds an MFA from Queens University of Charlotte and teaches creative writing. He lives in Long Beach, California. More of his writing can be found at danielromo.net.

Made in the USA
Middletown, DE
12 October 2020